SAVIOR
The Promise Fulfilled

LOVEGODGREATLY.COM

AT LOVE GOD GREATLY, YOU'LL FIND
REAL, AUTHENTIC WOMEN. WOMEN WHO
ARE IMPERFECT, YET FORGIVEN.

Women who desire less of us, and a whole lot
more of Jesus. Women who long to know God
through His Word, because we know that Truth
transforms and sets us free. Women who are
better together, saturated in God's Word and in
community with one another.

Welcome, friend. We're so glad you're here...

CONTENTS

WELCOME

We are glad you have decided to join us in this Bible study! First of all, please know that you have been prayed for! It is not a coincidence you are participating in this study.

Our prayer for you is simple: that you will grow closer to our Lord as you dig into His Word each and every day! As you develop the discipline of being in God's Word on a daily basis, our prayer is that you will fall in love with Him even more as you spend time reading from the Bible.

Each day before you read the assigned Scripture(s), pray and ask God to help you understand it. Invite Him to speak to you through His Word. Then listen. It's His job to speak to you, and it's your job to listen and obey.

Take time to read the verses over and over again. We are told in Proverbs to search and you will find: "Search for it like silver, and hunt for it like hidden treasure. Then you will understand" (Prov. 2:4–5 NCV).

All of us here at Love God Greatly can't wait for you to get started, and we hope to see you at the finish line. Endure, persevere, press on—and don't give up! Finish well what you are beginning today. We will be here every step of the way, cheering you on! We are in this together. Fight to rise early, to push back the stress of the day, to sit alone and spend time in God's Word! Let's see what God has in store for you in this study! Journey with us as we learn to love God greatly with our lives!

As you go through this study, join us in the following resources below:

Weekly Blog Posts •

Weekly Memory Verses •

Weekly Challenges •

Facebook, Twitter, Instagram •

LoveGodGreatly.com •

Hashtags: #LoveGodGreatly •

RESOURCES

Join Us

ONLINE

lovegodgreatly.com

STORE

lovegodgreatly.com/store

FACEBOOK

facebook.com/LoveGodGreatly

INSTAGRAM

instagram.com/lovegodgreatlyofficial

TWITTER

@_LoveGodGreatly

DOWNLOAD THE APP

CONTACT US

info@lovegodgreatly.com

CONNECT

#LoveGodGreatly

LOVE
GOD
GREATLY

Love God Greatly (LGG) is a beautiful community of women who use a variety of technology platforms to keep each other accountable in God's Word. We start with a simple Bible reading plan, but it doesn't stop there.

Some women gather in homes and churches locally, while others connect online with women across the globe. Whatever the method, we lovingly lock arms and unite for this purpose: to love God greatly with our lives.

Would you consider reaching out and doing this study with someone?

In today's fast-paced technology-driven world, it would be easy to study God's Word in an isolated environment that lacks encouragement or support, but that isn't the intention here at Love God Greatly. God created us to live in community with Him and with those around us.

We need each other, and we live life better together. Because of this, would you consider reaching out and doing this study with someone?

Rest assured we'll be studying right alongside you—learning with you, cheering for you, enjoying sweet fellowship, and smiling from ear to ear as we watch God unite women together—intentionally connecting hearts and minds for His glory.

So here's the challenge: call your mom, your sister, your grandma, the girl across the street, or the college friend across the country. Gather a group of girls from your church or workplace, or meet in a coffee shop with friends you have always wished you knew better.

Arm-in-arm and hand-in-hand, let's do this thing…together.

SOAP STUDY

HOW AND WHY TO SOAP

In this study we offer you a study journal to accompany the verses we are reading. This journal is designed to help you interact with God's Word and learn to dig deeper, encouraging you to slow down and reflect on what God is saying to you that day.

At Love God Greatly, we use the SOAP Bible study method. Before beginning, let's take a moment to define this method and share why we recommend using it during your quiet time in the following pages.

The most important ingredients in the SOAP method are your interaction with God's Word and your application of His Word to your life.

It's one thing to simply read Scripture. But when you interact with it, intentionally slowing down to really reflect on it, suddenly words start popping off the page. The SOAP method allows you to dig deeper into Scripture and see more than you would if you simply read the verses and then went on your merry way.

The most important ingredients in the SOAP method are your interaction with God's Word and your application of His Word to your life:

Blessed is the one who does not walk in step with the wicked or stand in the way that sinners take or sit in the company of mockers, but whose delight is in the law of the LORD, and who meditates on his law day and night. That person is like a tree planted by streams of water, which yields its fruit in season and whose leaf does not wither—whatever they do prospers. (Ps. 1:1–3, NIV)

Please take the time to SOAP through our Bible studies and see for yourself how much more you get from your daily reading.

You'll be amazed.

SOAP STUDY *(CONTINUED)*
WHAT DOES SOAP MEAN?

S STANDS FOR
SCRIPTURE

Physically write out the verses.

You'll be amazed at what God will reveal to you just by taking the time to slow down and write out what you are reading!

O STANDS FOR
OBSERVATION

What do you see in the verses that you're reading?

Who is the intended audience? Is there a repetition of words?

What words stand out to you?

MONDAY

READ
Colossians 1:5–8

SOAP
Colossians 1:5–8

Scripture

WRITE
OUT THE
SCRIPTURE
PASSAGE
FOR THE
DAY.

The faith and love that spring from the hope stored up for you in heaven and about which you have already heard in the true message of the gospel that has come to you. In the same way the gospel is bearing fruit and growing throughout the whole world just as it has been doing among you since the day you heard it and truly understood God's grace. You learned it from Epaphras, our dear fellow servant, who is a faithful minister of Christ on our behalf, and who also told us of your love in the Spirit.

Observations

WRITE
DOWN 1 OR 2
OBSERVATIONS
FROM THE
PASSAGE

When you combine faith and love, you get hope. We must remember that our hope is in heaven; it is yet to come. The gospel is the Word of truth. This gospel is continually bearing fruit and growing from the first day to the last. It just takes one person to change a whole community. Epaphras.

A STANDS FOR
APPLICATION

*This is when God's
Word becomes
personal.*

*What is God
saying to you today?*

*How can you apply
what you just read
to your own personal
life?*

*What changes do you
need to make? Is there
action you need to
take?*

Applications

WRITE
DOWN 1 OR 2
APPLICATIONS
FROM THE
PASSAGE.

God used one man, Epaphras, to change a whole town. I was reminded that we are simply called to tell others about Christ; it is God's job to spread the gospel, to grow it, and have it bear fruit. I felt today's verses were almost directly spoken to Love God Greatly women: The gospel is bearing fruit and growing throughout the whole world just as it has been doing among you since the day you heard it and truly understood God's grace.

Pray

WRITE OUT
A PRAYER
OVER WHAT
YOU LEARNED
FROM TODAY'S
PASSAGE.

Dear Lord, please help me to be an Epaphras, to tell others about You and then leave the results in Your loving hands. Please help me to understand and apply personally what I have read today to my life, thereby becoming more and more like You each and every day. Help me to live a life that bears the fruit of faith and love, anchoring my hope in heaven, not here on earth. Help me to remember that the best is yet to come!

P STANDS FOR **PRAYER**

Pray God's Word back to Him. Spend time thanking Him.

If He has revealed something to you during this time in His Word, pray about it.

If He has revealed some sin that is in your life, confess. And remember, He loves you dearly.

A RECIPE
FOR YOU
RED BRAISED PORK BELLY
(HONG SHAO ROU)

Ingredients

600 g Pork Belly (about 1.5 pounds)

2 tablespoons rock sugar

1 pod star anise

2 bay leaves

1 tablespoon soy sauce

2 tablespoons dark soy sauce

2 tablespoons shaoxing rice wine

Directions

- Cut the pork belly into thick pieces, about 1 inch long.

- Heat a wok over medium high heat. Once the wok is preheated, add 1 teaspoon of oil. This is to prevent the pork from sticking. Use a spatula to coat the bottom of the wok. Arrange the pork belly in a single layer and fry each side until slightly brown. Transfer to a plate and set aside.

- Clean the wok and reduce to medium heat. Add 2 tablespoons of water and 2 tablespoons of rock sugar.

- Once the sugar is starting to dissolve, add 1 teaspoon of oil and reduce the heat to low. Keep stirring until it turns brown. Then add in 1/4 cup hot water and bring just to a boil. Mix well and transfer to a bowl.

- Turn the heat to high, add 1 teaspoon oil, then add ginger, bay leaves, and star anise to the wok, cooking until fragrant. Then add soy sauce, dark soy sauce, rice wine and the sugar mixture.

- Once the sauce is boiling, return the pork belly to the wok and mix well.

- Add HOT (not cold) water to the wok. The water should cover most of the pork belly. Cover with a lid. Reduce the heat to a gentle simmer for 1.5 hours.

- Once the sauce is reduced to 1/4, turn the heat to high. Keep stirring as the sauce starts thickening. Be careful not to cook the pork for too long over high heat, or it will squeeze out the moisture and the pork will become dry.

- When the pork belly turns red and shiny, transfer to a plate and serve.

LGG CHINESE TESTIMONY

BI ZHAO, UNITED STATES

My name is Bi Zhao. I am a translator for the Chinese LGG team. I currently live in Indiana, US, with my husband and three kids. Our team now has 6 members with origins from mainland China, Taiwan, and Singapore. We are translating the study journal, reading plan and Bible verses for every six-week study. We also translate one blog post every Monday during each study. You can find both simplified and traditional Chinese versions of the Love God Greatly studies at www.lovegodgreatly.com, or on our Facebook page: "爱主更深事工".

God, only God, can do such a thing like this.

I joined the translation team in 2014. The Love God Greatly study materials appealed to me as simple but well-structured, and above all, rooted in the Word of God. The SOAP method (Scripture, Observation, Application, Prayer) provides an easy guideline to follow as I go through the Word every day. I adopted the method myself soon after I started translating. It allowed me to pay close attention to the Word, while at the same time leaving space for God to speak to me. Over the years, I've learned not only a method, but a habit, to stay humble and faithful in the pursuit of truth.

Growing up in the biggest city in China, Shanghai, I deeply feel the need for the Truth of God's Word for women in China. Like women everywhere else, they experience the fallen nature of the world on a daily basis and fight to find their own place. Many are driven by the motivation to excel, to achieve an identity by what they do, or how they look, or what they possess. Yet access to the Bible, Christian books, and study materials is still relatively scarce in China. As we translate, we pray that these materials will be used by God in ways that we cannot fathom. Though it is still impossible to reach women in mainland China on a large scale, we trust the mighty hands of God. We trust that He will use all resources and opportunities to reach women and rescue one after another. God is faithful. Through the Facebook page, the number of women reached by LGG is growing. We are called to be faithful and persevere; and we are thankful for the opportunity to serve in this way.

Here is a little story about how God amazes us by His sovereignty in using LGG Chinese materials. I joined the

Love God Greatly intensive in Dallas last September. The intensive is an event to train the translators of various languages and to build up relationships among each other and the team. Upon my arrival, my lovely roommate, Viola from Hungary grabbed me and said: "You are the Chinese translator, right? You know what, there is a group of Chinese women in Budapest using your translation right now as Bible study material!" It took me a few seconds to reflect: Budapest, Hungary! Chinese LGG Bible studies! The next moment I was all in awe and praising God! How could we ever imagine that the translation we did on our little laptop, the translation that we don't even know where it would travel to, would one day reach a group of women, that we never think of! But God, only God, can do such a thing like this. Imagining the women of different corners of the world who might be holding a Bible and a study journal right now makes me humble and thankful! And we believe He is still in the business; He does not stop working!

Praise be to our Lord Jesus Christ!

To connect with LGG Chinese Branch:

- facebook.com/LGGChinese
- compassionforhim@gmail.com

Do you know someone who could use our *Love God Greatly* Bible studies in Chinese? If so, make sure and tell them about LGG Chinese and all the amazing Bible study resources we provide to help equip them with God's Word!!!

SAVIOR

The Promise Fulfilled

Let's Begin

INTRODUCTION

SAVIOR

Christmas is coming! Are you prepared for the busyness of the season? The holiday is packed with shopping, music, lights, decorations, school plays and very long to-do lists. We have to think about gatherings, presents, menus. There are cards to send, emails to write, pictures to take, family and friends to visit. We see our schedules and panic, knowing that it´s impossible to do all the things on our list.

In the middle of our very busy days, it´s easy to forget what we really celebrate in Christmas: We celebrate Jesus. We celebrate His coming.

The world turned upside down when Jesus was born. All the Old Testament prophecies about the coming of the long-awaited Messiah were fulfilled with the birth of Jesus. The Savior became flesh. Jesus incarnated Himself to give us life, to have our sins forgiven, and to give us the opportunity to be saved of the judgment we deserve.

The story of Christmas is full of ordinary people who experienced extraordinary circumstances. We see angels talking to Zechariah, Mary, and Joseph. Angels singing in choir fill the night with praise while the shepherds tend to their flocks. A bright star guides the Magi to Bethlehem, civilian authorities are used by God as a part of His eternal plan. We see miracles. The miracle of John the Baptist conceived in Elizabeth´s old age. And, over all, the miracle of the incarnation of Christ. A young virgin giving birth to the second person of the Trinity.

"And the angel said to them, "Fear not, for behold, I bring you good news of great joy that will be for all the people. For unto you is born this day in the city of David a Savior, who is Christ the Lord."
– Luke 2:10-11

We celebrate the good news of Jesus´ birth. This was news of great joy and would be for all the people, in three very special ways:

- Jesus is the Savior who delivers us from sin and death (Matthew 1:21).

- He is the human Christ, the Messiah who fulfills the Law and the Prophets, showing that God is faithful (Matthew 5:17).

- He is the Lord who has entered our world in an indivisible, eternal bond of God and man; *Emmanuel, God with us* (Matthew 1:23).

As we enjoy the season, the parties, the presents, the time with friends and family, let's make Christmas a celebration of His coming!

READING PLAN

WEEK 1
THE FORETELLING OF HIS COMING

Monday – Out of darkness
READ: Isaiah 9:1-7; Ephesians 5:8-10
SOAP: Isaiah 9:2

Tuesday – A branch from the stump of Jesse
READ: Isaiah 11:1-10; Matthew 1:5-6
SOAP: Isaiah 11:1

Wednesday – The Messiah will be born to forgive our sins
READ: Isaiah 7:14-17; Isaiah 40:1-2
SOAP: Isaiah 7:14

Thursday – Nothing is too little in the hands of the Lord
READ: Micah 5:2-4; John 7:42
SOAP: Micah 5:2

Friday – The King is bringing Salvation
READ: Zechariah 9:9-10; Luke 19:35-38
SOAP: Zechariah 9:9

WEEK 2
THE REASON FOR HIS COMING

Monday – To set an example of humility
READ: Philippians 2:5-8
SOAP: Philippians 2:8

Tuesday – To redeem humanity
READ: Galatians 4:4-7; 1 Peter 1:17-21
SOAP: Galatians 4:4-5

Wednesday – To allow us to see the Word becoming flesh
READ: John 1:1-5, 14; 1 Timothy 3:16
SOAP: John 1:14

Thursday – To allow us to have life in His Name
READ: John 20:30-31; John 3:14-15
SOAP: John 20:31

Friday – To show the very nature of God
READ: Hebrews 1:1-4; Colossians 1:15-16
SOAP: Hebrews 1:3

WEEK 3
THE PREPARATION OF HIS COMING

Monday – Making the people ready for the Lord – Zechariah and Elizabeth.
READ: Malachi 3:1; Luke 1:13-17
SOAP: Luke 1:17

Tuesday – The Kingdom of Heaven is at hand – John the Baptist
READ: Matthew 3:1-3; Luke 1:41
SOAP: Matthew 3:2

Wednesday – You shall call His name Jesus - Mary
READ: Luke 1:26-33
SOAP: Luke 1:30-31

Thursday – The Son of God - Mary
READ: Luke 1:34-38; Matthew 26:63, 64
SOAP: Luke 1:35

Friday – Immanuel, God with us - Joseph
READ: Matthew 1:18-25
SOAP: Matthew 1:23

WEEK 4
THE JOY OF HIS COMING

Monday – A decree to obey
READ: Luke 2:1-5
SOAP: Luke 2:3-4

Tuesday – A baby in a manger
READ: Luke 2:6-7
SOAP: Luke 2:6-7

Wednesday – Giving Him the Glory
READ: Luke 2:8-14
SOAP: Luke 2:10-11

Thursday – Worship the King
READ: Luke 2:15-20; 1 Corinthians 10:31
SOAP: Luke 2:20

Friday – Presents for the King
READ: Matthew 2:9-12; Revelation 15:4
SOAP: Matthew 2:11-12

YOUR GOALS

We believe it's important to write out goals for this study. Take some time now and write three goals you would like to focus on as you begin to rise each day and dig into God's Word. Make sure and refer back to these goals throughout the next weeks to help you stay focused. You can do it!

1.

2.

3.

Signature:

Date:

WEEK 1

The Foretelling of His coming

Rejoice greatly, O daughter of Zion!

Shout aloud, O daughter of Jerusalem!

Behold, your king is coming to you;

righteous and having salvation is he,

humble and mounted on a donkey,

on a colt, the foal of a donkey.

ZECHARIAH 9:9

PRAYER

Prayer focus for this week:
Spend time praying for your family members.

MONDAY

TUESDAY

WEDNESDAY

THURSDAY

FRIDAY

CHALLENGE

You can find this listed in our Monday blog post.

MONDAY
Scripture for Week 1

Isaiah 9:1-7

1 But there will be no gloom for her who was in anguish. In the former time he brought into contempt the land of Zebulun and the land of Naphtali, but in the latter time he has made glorious the way of the sea, the land beyond the Jordan, Galilee of the nations.

2 The people who walked in darkness
    have seen a great light;
those who dwelt in a land of deep darkness,
    on them has light shone.
3 You have multiplied the nation;
    you have increased its joy;
they rejoice before you
    as with joy at the harvest,
    as they are glad when they divide the spoil.
4 For the yoke of his burden,
    and the staff for his shoulder,
    the rod of his oppressor,
    you have broken as on the day of Midian.
5 For every boot of the tramping warrior in battle tumult
    and every garment rolled in blood
    will be burned as fuel for the fire.
6 For to us a child is born,
    to us a son is given;
and the government shall be upon his shoulder,
    and his name shall be called
Wonderful Counselor, Mighty God,
    Everlasting Father, Prince of Peace.
7 Of the increase of his government and of peace
    there will be no end,
on the throne of David and over his kingdom,
    to establish it and to uphold it
with justice and with righteousness
    from this time forth and forevermore.
The zeal of the Lord of hosts will do this.

Ephesians 5:8-10

8 for at one time you were darkness, but now you are light in the Lord. Walk as children of light 9 (for the fruit of light is found in all that is good and right and true),10 and try to discern what is pleasing to the Lord.

MONDAY

READ:
Isaiah 9:1-7; Ephesians 5:8-10

SOAP:
Isaiah 9:2

Scripture

WRITE
OUT THE
SCRIPTURE
PASSAGE
FOR THE
DAY.

Observations

WRITE
DOWN 1 OR 2
OBSERVATIONS
FROM THE
PASSAGE.

Applications

WRITE
DOWN 1 OR 2
APPLICATIONS
FROM THE
PASSAGE.

Pray

WRITE OUT
A PRAYER
OVER WHAT
YOU LEARNED
FROM TODAY'S
PASSAGE.

TUESDAY
Scripture for Week 1

Isaiah 11:1-10
1 There shall come forth a shoot from the stump of Jesse,
  and a branch from his roots shall bear fruit.
2 And the Spirit of the Lord shall rest upon him,
  the Spirit of wisdom and understanding,
  the Spirit of counsel and might,
  the Spirit of knowledge and the fear of the Lord.
3 And his delight shall be in the fear of the Lord.
He shall not judge by what his eyes see,
  or decide disputes by what his ears hear,
4 but with righteousness he shall judge the poor,
  and decide with equity for the meek of the earth;
and he shall strike the earth with the rod of his mouth,
  and with the breath of his lips he shall kill the wicked.
5 Righteousness shall be the belt of his waist,
  and faithfulness the belt of his loins.
6 The wolf shall dwell with the lamb,
  and the leopard shall lie down with the young goat,
and the calf and the lion and the fattened calf together;
  and a little child shall lead them.
7 The cow and the bear shall graze;
  their young shall lie down together;
  and the lion shall eat straw like the ox.
8 The nursing child shall play over the hole of the cobra,
  and the weaned child shall put his hand on the adder's den.
9 They shall not hurt or destroy
  in all my holy mountain;
for the earth shall be full of the knowledge of the Lord
  as the waters cover the sea.

10 In that day the root of Jesse, who shall stand as a signal for the peoples—of him shall the nations inquire, and his resting place shall be glorious.

Matthew 1:5-6
5 and Salmon the father of Boaz by Rahab, and Boaz the father of Obed by Ruth, and Obed the father of Jesse, 6 and Jesse the father of David the king.

And David was the father of Solomon by the wife of Uriah,

TUESDAY

READ:
Isaiah 11:1-10; Matthew 1:5-6

SOAP:
Isaiah 11:1

Scripture

WRITE
OUT THE
SCRIPTURE
PASSAGE
FOR THE
DAY.

Observations

WRITE
DOWN 1 OR 2
OBSERVATIONS
FROM THE
PASSAGE.

Applications

WRITE
DOWN 1 OR 2
APPLICATIONS
FROM THE
PASSAGE.

Pray

WRITE OUT
A PRAYER
OVER WHAT
YOU LEARNED
FROM TODAY'S
PASSAGE.

WEDNESDAY
Scripture for Week 1

Isaiah 7:14-17
14 Therefore the Lord himself will give you a sign. Behold,
the virgin shall conceive and bear a son, and shall call his
name Immanuel. 15 He shall eat curds and honey when he knows
how to refuse the evil and choose the good. 16 For before the boy
knows how to refuse the evil and choose the good, the land whose
two kings you dread will be deserted. 17 The Lord will bring upon
you and upon your people and upon your father's house such
days as have not come since the day that Ephraim departed from
Judah—the king of Assyria!"

Isaiah 40:1-2
1 Comfort, comfort my people, says your God.
2 Speak tenderly to Jerusalem,
    and cry to her
that her warfare is ended,
    that her iniquity is pardoned,
that she has received from the Lord's hand
    double for all her sins.

WEDNESDAY

READ:
Isaiah 7:14-17; Isaiah 40:1-2

SOAP:
Isaiah 7:14

Scripture

WRITE
OUT THE
SCRIPTURE
PASSAGE
FOR THE
DAY.

Observations

WRITE
DOWN 1 OR 2
OBSERVATIONS
FROM THE
PASSAGE.

Applications

WRITE
DOWN 1 OR 2
APPLICATIONS
FROM THE
PASSAGE.

Pray

WRITE OUT
A PRAYER
OVER WHAT
YOU LEARNED
FROM TODAY'S
PASSAGE.

THURSDAY
Scripture for Week 1

Micah 5:2-4

2 But you, O Bethlehem Ephrathah,
   who are too little to be among the clans of Judah,
from you shall come forth for me
   one who is to be ruler in Israel,
whose coming forth is from of old,
   from ancient days.
3 Therefore he shall give them up until the time
   when she who is in labor has given birth;
then the rest of his brothers shall return
   to the people of Israel.
4 And he shall stand and shepherd his flock in the strength of
the Lord,
   in the majesty of the name of the Lord his God.
And they shall dwell secure, for now he shall be great
   to the ends of the earth.

John 7:42

42 Has not the Scripture said that the Christ comes from the
offspring of David, and comes from Bethlehem, the village where
David was?"

THURSDAY

READ:
Micah 5:2-4; John 7:42

SOAP:
Micah 5:2

Scripture

WRITE
OUT THE
SCRIPTURE
PASSAGE
FOR THE
DAY.

Observations

WRITE
DOWN 1 OR 2
OBSERVATIONS
FROM THE
PASSAGE.

Applications

WRITE
DOWN 1 OR 2
APPLICATIONS
FROM THE
PASSAGE.

Pray

WRITE OUT
A PRAYER
OVER WHAT
YOU LEARNED
FROM TODAY'S
PASSAGE.

FRIDAY

Scripture for Week 1

Zechariah 9:9-10

9 Rejoice greatly, O daughter of Zion!
  Shout aloud, O daughter of Jerusalem!
Behold, your king is coming to you;
  righteous and having salvation is he,
humble and mounted on a donkey,
  on a colt, the foal of a donkey.
10 I will cut off the chariot from Ephraim
  and the war horse from Jerusalem;
and the battle bow shall be cut off,
  and he shall speak peace to the nations;
his rule shall be from sea to sea,
  and from the River to the ends of the earth.

Luke 19:35-38

35 And they brought it to Jesus, and throwing their cloaks on the colt, they set Jesus on it. 36 And as he rode along, they spread their cloaks on the road. 37 As he was drawing near—already on the way down the Mount of Olives—the whole multitude of his disciples began to rejoice and praise God with a loud voice for all the mighty works that they had seen, 38 saying, "Blessed is the King who comes in the name of the Lord! Peace in heaven and glory in the highest!"

FRIDAY

READ:
Zechariah 9:9-10; Luke 19:35-38

SOAP:
Zechariah 9:9

Scripture

WRITE
OUT THE
SCRIPTURE
PASSAGE
FOR THE
DAY.

Observations

WRITE
DOWN 1 OR 2
OBSERVATIONS
FROM THE
PASSAGE.

Applications

WRITE
DOWN 1 OR 2
APPLICATIONS
FROM THE
PASSAGE.

Pray

WRITE OUT
A PRAYER
OVER WHAT
YOU LEARNED
FROM TODAY'S
PASSAGE.

REFLECTION
QUESTIONS

1. Why do people need the Light of Jesus? How can we live in His light?

2. Do you see the Bible as a whole or as separate stories? Write about how reading Isaiah's prophecy allows you to weave all of Scripture together.

3. How does knowing that God has it all together comforts your heart and helps you get through dark days?

4. The small town of Bethlehem was unlikely to be considered as the place where the Messiah would be born. Do you feel "small" in any aspect of your life? How can God use you?

5. The coming of the King to save the world was a reason to rejoice. Look up four verses that talk about joy in Scripture.

NOTES

WEEK 2

The Reason for His coming

And the Word became flesh and dwelt among us, and we have seen his glory, glory as of the only Son from the Father, full of grace and truth

JOHN 1:14

PRAYER

Prayer focus for this week:
Spend time praying for your country.

MONDAY

TUESDAY

WEDNESDAY

THURSDAY

FRIDAY

CHALLENGE

You can find this listed in our Monday blog post.

46

MONDAY
Scripture for Week 2

Philippians 2:5-8
5 Have this mind among yourselves, which is yours in Christ
Jesus, 6 who, though he was in the form of God, did not count
equality with God a thing to be grasped, 7 but emptied himself,
by taking the form of a servant, being born in the likeness of
men. 8 And being found in human form, he humbled himself
by becoming obedient to the point of death, even death on a cross.

MONDAY

READ:
Philippians 2:5-8

SOAP:
Philippians 2:8

Scripture

WRITE
OUT THE
SCRIPTURE
PASSAGE
FOR THE
DAY.

Observations

WRITE
DOWN 1 OR 2
OBSERVATIONS
FROM THE
PASSAGE.

Applications

WRITE
DOWN 1 OR 2
APPLICATIONS
FROM THE
PASSAGE.

Pray

WRITE OUT
A PRAYER
OVER WHAT
YOU LEARNED
FROM TODAY'S
PASSAGE.

TUESDAY
Scripture for Week 2

Galatians 4:4-7
4 But when the fullness of time had come, God sent forth his
Son, born of woman, born under the law, 5 to redeem those
who were under the law, so that we might receive adoption as
sons. 6 And because you are sons, God has sent the Spirit of his Son
into our hearts, crying, "Abba! Father!" 7 So you are no longer a
slave, but a son, and if a son, then an heir through God.

1 Peter 1:17-21
17 And if you call on him as Father who judges impartially
according to each one's deeds, conduct yourselves with fear
throughout the time of your exile, 18 knowing that you were
ransomed from the futile ways inherited from your forefathers,
not with perishable things such as silver or gold, 19 but with the
precious blood of Christ, like that of a lamb without blemish or
spot. 20 He was foreknown before the foundation of the world
but was made manifest in the last times for the sake of you 21 who
through him are believers in God, who raised him from the dead
and gave him glory, so that your faith and hope are in God.

TUESDAY

READ:
Galatians 4:4-7; 1 Peter 1:17-21

SOAP:
Galatians 4:4-5

Scripture

WRITE
OUT THE
SCRIPTURE
PASSAGE
FOR THE
DAY.

Observations

WRITE
DOWN 1 OR 2
OBSERVATIONS
FROM THE
PASSAGE.

Applications

WRITE
DOWN 1 OR 2
APPLICATIONS
FROM THE
PASSAGE.

Pray

WRITE OUT
A PRAYER
OVER WHAT
YOU LEARNED
FROM TODAY'S
PASSAGE.

WEDNESDAY
Scripture for Week 2

John 1:1-5, 14

1 In the beginning was the Word, and the Word was with God, and the Word was God. 2 He was in the beginning with God. 3 All things were made through him, and without him was not any thing made that was made. 4 In him was life,[a] and the life was the light of men. 5 The light shines in the darkness, and the darkness has not overcome it.

14 And the Word became flesh and dwelt among us, and we have seen his glory, glory as of the only Son from the Father, full of grace and truth.

1 Timothy 3:16

16 Great indeed, we confess, is the mystery of godliness:
He was manifested in the flesh,
   vindicated by the Spirit,
     seen by angels,
proclaimed among the nations,
   believed on in the world,
     taken up in glory.

WEDNESDAY

READ:
John 1:1-5, 14; 1 Timothy 3:16

SOAP:
John 1:14

Scripture

WRITE
OUT THE
SCRIPTURE
PASSAGE
FOR THE
DAY.

Observations

WRITE
DOWN 1 OR 2
OBSERVATIONS
FROM THE
PASSAGE.

Applications

WRITE
DOWN 1 OR 2
APPLICATIONS
FROM THE
PASSAGE.

Pray

WRITE OUT
A PRAYER
OVER WHAT
YOU LEARNED
FROM TODAY'S
PASSAGE.

THURSDAY
Scripture for Week 2

John 20:30-31
30 Now Jesus did many other signs in the presence of the disciples, which are not written in this book; 31 but these are written so that you may believe that Jesus is the Christ, the Son of God, and that by believing you may have life in his name.

John 3:14-15
14 And as Moses lifted up the serpent in the wilderness, so must the Son of Man be lifted up, 15 that whoever believes in him may have eternal life.

THURSDAY

READ:
John 20:30-31; John 3:14-15

SOAP:
John 20:31

Scripture

WRITE
OUT THE
SCRIPTURE
PASSAGE
FOR THE
DAY.

Observations

WRITE
DOWN 1 OR 2
OBSERVATIONS
FROM THE
PASSAGE.

Applications

WRITE
DOWN 1 OR 2
APPLICATIONS
FROM THE
PASSAGE.

Pray

WRITE OUT
A PRAYER
OVER WHAT
YOU LEARNED
FROM TODAY'S
PASSAGE.

FRIDAY
Scripture for Week 2

Hebrews 1:1-4
1 Long ago, at many times and in many ways, God spoke to our
fathers by the prophets, 2 but in these last days he has spoken to
us by his Son, whom he appointed the heir of all things, through
whom also he created the world. 3 He is the radiance of the glory
of God and the exact imprint of his nature, and he upholds the
universe by the word of his power. After making purification for
sins, he sat down at the right hand of the Majesty on high, 4 having
become as much superior to angels as the name he has inherited is
more excellent than theirs.

Colossians 1:15-16
15 He is the image of the invisible God, the firstborn of all
creation. 16 For by him all things were created, in heaven and on
earth, visible and invisible, whether thrones or dominions or rulers
or authorities—all things were created through him and for him.

FRIDAY

READ:
Hebrews 1:1-4; Colossians 1:15-16

SOAP:
Hebrews 1:3

Scripture

WRITE
OUT THE
SCRIPTURE
PASSAGE
FOR THE
DAY.

Observations

WRITE
DOWN 1 OR 2
OBSERVATIONS
FROM THE
PASSAGE.

Applications

WRITE
DOWN 1 OR 2
APPLICATIONS
FROM THE
PASSAGE.

Pray

WRITE OUT
A PRAYER
OVER WHAT
YOU LEARNED
FROM TODAY'S
PASSAGE.

REFLECTION QUESTIONS

1. How does knowing that Jesus took the form of a servant and emptied Himself affect your daily life?

2. What does it mean to be an heir of God? How are we to conduct ourselves as daughters of the King?

3. John 1:1 is a short verse but it's full of meaning. What does it says about Jesus – the Word?

4. What was the importance of registering Jesus' miracles and putting them in a book?

5. What do we learn about Jesus in these verses?

NOTES

WEEK 3

The Preparation of His coming

Repent, for the kingdom of heaven is at hand

MATTHEW 3:2

PRAYER

Prayer focus for this week:
Spend time praying for your friends.

MONDAY

TUESDAY

WEDNESDAY

THURSDAY

FRIDAY

CHALLENGE

You can find this listed in our Monday blog post.

MONDAY
Scripture for Week 3

Malachi 3:1

1 "Behold, I send my messenger, and he will prepare the way before me. And the Lord whom you seek will suddenly come to his temple; and the messenger of the covenant in whom you delight, behold, he is coming, says the Lord of hosts.

Luke 1:13-17

13 But the angel said to him, "Do not be afraid, Zechariah, for your prayer has been heard, and your wife Elizabeth will bear you a son, and you shall call his name John. 14 And you will have joy and gladness, and many will rejoice at his birth,15 for he will be great before the Lord. And he must not drink wine or strong drink, and he will be filled with the Holy Spirit, even from his mother's womb. 16 And he will turn many of the children of Israel to the Lord their God, 17 and he will go before him in the spirit and power of Elijah, to turn the hearts of the fathers to the children, and the disobedient to the wisdom of the just, to make ready for the Lord a people prepared."

MONDAY

READ:
Malachi 3:1; Luke 1:13-17

SOAP:
Luke 1:17

Scripture

WRITE
OUT THE
SCRIPTURE
PASSAGE
FOR THE
DAY.

Observations

WRITE
DOWN 1 OR 2
OBSERVATIONS
FROM THE
PASSAGE.

Applications

WRITE
DOWN 1 OR 2
APPLICATIONS
FROM THE
PASSAGE.

Pray

WRITE OUT
A PRAYER
OVER WHAT
YOU LEARNED
FROM TODAY'S
PASSAGE.

TUESDAY
Scripture for Week 3

Matthew 3:1-3
1 In those days John the Baptist came preaching in the wilderness of Judea,2 "Repent, for the kingdom of heaven is at hand." 3 For this is he who was spoken of by the prophet Isaiah when he said,

"The voice of one crying in the wilderness:
'Prepare the way of the Lord;
    make his paths straight.'"

Luke 1:41
41 And when Elizabeth heard the greeting of Mary, the baby leaped in her womb. And Elizabeth was filled with the Holy Spirit,

TUESDAY

READ:
Matthew 3:1-3; Luke 1:41

SOAP:
Matthew 3:2

Scripture

WRITE
OUT THE
SCRIPTURE
PASSAGE
FOR THE
DAY.

Observations

WRITE
DOWN 1 OR 2
OBSERVATIONS
FROM THE
PASSAGE.

Applications

WRITE
DOWN 1 OR 2
APPLICATIONS
FROM THE
PASSAGE.

Pray

WRITE OUT
A PRAYER
OVER WHAT
YOU LEARNED
FROM TODAY'S
PASSAGE.

WEDNESDAY
Scripture for Week 3

Luke 1:26-33

26 In the sixth month the angel Gabriel was sent from God to a city of Galilee named Nazareth, 27 to a virgin betrothed to a man whose name was Joseph, of the house of David. And the virgin's name was Mary. 28 And he came to her and said, "Greetings, O favored one, the Lord is with you!" 29 But she was greatly troubled at the saying, and tried to discern what sort of greeting this might be.30 And the angel said to her, "Do not be afraid, Mary, for you have found favor with God. 31 And behold, you will conceive in your womb and bear a son, and you shall call his name Jesus. 32 He will be great and will be called the Son of the Most High. And the Lord God will give to him the throne of his father David, 33 and he will reign over the house of Jacob forever, and of his kingdom there will be no end."

WEDNESDAY

READ:
Luke 1:26-33

SOAP:
Luke 1:30-31

Scripture

WRITE
OUT THE
SCRIPTURE
PASSAGE
FOR THE
DAY.

Observations

WRITE
DOWN 1 OR 2
OBSERVATIONS
FROM THE
PASSAGE.

Applications

WRITE
DOWN 1 OR 2
APPLICATIONS
FROM THE
PASSAGE.

Pray

WRITE OUT
A PRAYER
OVER WHAT
YOU LEARNED
FROM TODAY'S
PASSAGE.

THURSDAY

Scripture for Week 3

Luke 1:34-38

34 And Mary said to the angel, "How will this be, since I am a virgin?"

35 And the angel answered her, "The Holy Spirit will come upon you, and the power of the Most High will overshadow you; therefore the child to be born will be called holy—the Son of God. 36 And behold, your relative Elizabeth in her old age has also conceived a son, and this is the sixth month with her who was called barren. 37 For nothing will be impossible with God." 38 And Mary said, "Behold, I am the servant of the Lord; let it be to me according to your word." And the angel departed from her.

Matthew 26:63, 64

63 But Jesus remained silent. And the high priest said to him, "I adjure you by the living God, tell us if you are the Christ, the Son of God." 64 Jesus said to him, "You have said so. But I tell you, from now on you will see the Son of Man seated at the right hand of Power and coming on the clouds of heaven."

THURSDAY

READ:
Luke 1:34-38; Matthew 26:63, 64

SOAP:
Luke 1:35

Scripture

WRITE
OUT THE
SCRIPTURE
PASSAGE
FOR THE
DAY.

Observations

WRITE
DOWN 1 OR 2
OBSERVATIONS
FROM THE
PASSAGE.

Applications

WRITE
DOWN 1 OR 2
APPLICATIONS
FROM THE
PASSAGE.

Pray

WRITE OUT
A PRAYER
OVER WHAT
YOU LEARNED
FROM TODAY'S
PASSAGE.

FRIDAY

Scripture for Week 3

Matthew 1:18-25

18 Now the birth of Jesus Chris] took place in this way. When
his mother Mary had been betrothed to Joseph, before they
came together she was found to be with child from the
Holy Spirit. 19 And her husband Joseph, being a just man
and unwilling to put her to shame, resolved to divorce her
quietly. 20 But as he considered these things, behold, an angel of
the Lord appeared to him in a dream, saying, "Joseph, son of David,
do not fear to take Mary as your wife, for that which is conceived
in her is from the Holy Spirit. 21 She will bear a son, and you
shall call his name Jesus, for he will save his people from their
sins." 22 All this took place to fulfill what the Lord had spoken by
the prophet:

23 "Behold, the virgin shall conceive and bear a son,
    and they shall call his name Immanuel"

(which means, God with us). 24 When Joseph woke from sleep,
he did as the angel of the Lord commanded him: he took his
wife, 25 but knew her not until she had given birth to a son.
And he called his name Jesus.

FRIDAY

READ:
Matthew 1:18-25

SOAP:
Matthew 1:23

Scripture

WRITE
OUT THE
SCRIPTURE
PASSAGE
FOR THE
DAY.

Observations

WRITE
DOWN 1 OR 2
OBSERVATIONS
FROM THE
PASSAGE.

Applications

WRITE
DOWN 1 OR 2
APPLICATIONS
FROM THE
PASSAGE.

Pray

WRITE OUT
A PRAYER
OVER WHAT
YOU LEARNED
FROM TODAY'S
PASSAGE.

REFLECTION QUESTIONS

1. How is the prophecy in Malachi fulfilled in Luke's account?

2. What was John the Baptist doing in the wilderness?

3. What do these verses tell you about Mary?

4. What would have been your answer to the angel's speech? Do you think you would have answered, like Mary, "I am the servant of the Lord; let it be to me according to your word."? What aspects of your life do you need to surrender to God?

5. What do these verses tell you about Joseph?

NOTES

WEEK 4

The Joy of His Coming

---

*"Glory to God in the highest,
and on earth peace among those
with whom he is pleased!"*

LUKE 2:14

PRAYER

WRITE DOWN YOUR PRAYER REQUESTS
AND PRAISES FOR EACH DAY.

Prayer focus for this week:
Spend time praying for your church.

MONDAY

TUESDAY

WEDNESDAY

THURSDAY

FRIDAY

CHALLENGE

You can find this listed in our Monday blog post.

MONDAY
Scripture for Week 4

Luke 2:1-5

1 In those days a decree went out from Caesar Augustus that all the world should be registered. 2 This was the first registration when Quirinius was governor of Syria. 3 And all went to be registered, each to his own town. 4 And Joseph also went up from Galilee, from the town of Nazareth, to Judea, to the city of David, which is called Bethlehem, because he was of the house and lineage of David, 5 to be registered with Mary, his betrothed, who was with child.

MONDAY

READ:
Luke 2:1-5

SOAP:
Luke 2:3-4

Scripture

WRITE
OUT THE
SCRIPTURE
PASSAGE
FOR THE
DAY.

Observations

WRITE
DOWN 1 OR 2
OBSERVATIONS
FROM THE
PASSAGE.

Applications

WRITE
DOWN 1 OR 2
APPLICATIONS
FROM THE
PASSAGE.

Pray

WRITE OUT
A PRAYER
OVER WHAT
YOU LEARNED
FROM TODAY'S
PASSAGE.

TUESDAY
Scripture for Week 4

Luke 2:6-7
6 And while they were there, the time came for her to give
birth. 7 And she gave birth to her firstborn son and wrapped him
in swaddling cloths and laid him in a manger, because there was no
place for them in the inn.

TUESDAY

READ:
Luke 2:6-7

SOAP:
Luke 2:6-7

Scripture

WRITE
OUT THE
SCRIPTURE
PASSAGE
FOR THE
DAY.

Observations

WRITE
DOWN 1 OR 2
OBSERVATIONS
FROM THE
PASSAGE.

Applications

WRITE
DOWN 1 OR 2
APPLICATIONS
FROM THE
PASSAGE.

Pray

WRITE OUT
A PRAYER
OVER WHAT
YOU LEARNED
FROM TODAY'S
PASSAGE.

WEDNESDAY
Scripture for Week 4

Luke 2:8-14

8 And in the same region there were shepherds out in the field, keeping watch over their flock by night. 9 And an angel of the Lord appeared to them, and the glory of the Lord shone around them, and they were filled with great fear. 10 And the angel said to them, "Fear not, for behold, I bring you good news of great joy that will be for all the people. 11 For unto you is born this day in the city of David a Savior, who is Christ the Lord. 12 And this will be a sign for you: you will find a baby wrapped in swaddling cloths and lying in a manger." 13 And suddenly there was with the angel a multitude of the heavenly host praising God and saying,

14 "Glory to God in the highest,
    and on earth peace among those with whom he is pleased!"

WEDNESDAY

READ:
Luke 2:8-14

SOAP:
Luke 2:10-11

Scripture

WRITE
OUT THE
SCRIPTURE
PASSAGE
FOR THE
DAY.

Observations

WRITE
DOWN 1 OR 2
OBSERVATIONS
FROM THE
PASSAGE.

Applications

WRITE
DOWN 1 OR 2
APPLICATIONS
FROM THE
PASSAGE.

Pray

WRITE OUT
A PRAYER
OVER WHAT
YOU LEARNED
FROM TODAY'S
PASSAGE.

THURSDAY
Scripture for Week 4

Luke 2:15-20
15 When the angels went away from them into heaven, the shepherds said to one another, "Let us go over to Bethlehem and see this thing that has happened, which the Lord has made known to us." 16 And they went with haste and found Mary and Joseph, and the baby lying in a manger. 17 And when they saw it, they made known the saying that had been told them concerning this child. 18 And all who heard it wondered at what the shepherds told them. 19 But Mary treasured up all these things, pondering them in her heart. 20 And the shepherds returned, glorifying and praising God for all they had heard and seen, as it had been told them.

1 Corinthians 10:31
31 So, whether you eat or drink, or whatever you do, do all to the glory of God.

THURSDAY

Scripture

Observations

Applications

WRITE
DOWN 1 OR 2
APPLICATIONS
FROM THE
PASSAGE.

Pray

WRITE OUT
A PRAYER
OVER WHAT
YOU LEARNED
FROM TODAY'S
PASSAGE.

FRIDAY
Scripture for Week 4

Matthew 2:9-12
9 After listening to the king, they went on their way. And behold, the star that they had seen when it rose went before them until it came to rest over the place where the child was. 10 When they saw the star, they rejoiced exceedingly with great joy.11 And going into the house, they saw the child with Mary his mother, and they fell down and worshiped him. Then, opening their treasures, they offered him gifts, gold and frankincense and myrrh. 12 And being warned in a dream not to return to Herod, they departed to their own country by another way.

Revelation 15:4
4 Who will not fear, O Lord,
    and glorify your name?
For you alone are holy.
    All nations will come
    and worship you,
for your righteous acts have been revealed."

FRIDAY

READ:
Matthew 2:9-12; Revelation 15:4

SOAP:
Matthew 2:11-12

Scripture

WRITE
OUT THE
SCRIPTURE
PASSAGE
FOR THE
DAY.

Observations

WRITE
DOWN 1 OR 2
OBSERVATIONS
FROM THE
PASSAGE.

Applications

WRITE
DOWN 1 OR 2
APPLICATIONS
FROM THE
PASSAGE.

Pray

WRITE OUT
A PRAYER
OVER WHAT
YOU LEARNED
FROM TODAY'S
PASSAGE.

REFLECTION
QUESTIONS

1. What do today's verses tell you about God's Sovereignty?

2. Does Jesus have enough room in your life? How can you make more room for Him?

3. The good news of great joy (the Gospel) is for all the people. With whom can you share this news today?

4. How can you bring glory to God in your life?

5. This Christmas, instead of thinking about the presents you are about to receive, think about the "presents" that you can give Jesus.

NOTES

KNOW THESE TRUTHS
from God's Word

God loves you.
Even when you're feeling unworthy and like the world is stacked against you, God loves you - yes, you - and He has created you for great purpose.

God's Word says, "God so loved the world that He gave His one and only Son, Jesus, that whoever believes in Him shall not perish, but have eternal life" (John 3:16).

Our sin separates us from God.
We are all sinners by nature and by choice, and because of this we are separated from God, who is holy.

God's Word says, "All have sinned and fall short of the glory of God" (Romans 3:23).

Jesus died so that you might have life.
The consequence of sin is death, but your story doesn't have to end there! God's free gift of salvation is available to us because Jesus took the penalty for our sin when He died on the cross.

God's Word says, "For the wages of sin is death, but the free gift of God is eternal life in Christ Jesus our Lord" (Romans 6:23); "God demonstrates His own love toward us, in that while we were yet sinners, Christ died for us" (Romans 5:8).

Jesus lives!
Death could not hold Him, and three days after His body was placed in the tomb Jesus rose again, defeating sin and death forever! He lives today in heaven and is preparing a place in eternity for all who believe in Him.

God's Word says, "In my Father's house are many rooms. If it were not so, would I have told you that I go to prepare a place for you? And if I go and prepare a place for you, I will come again and will take you to myself, that where I am you may be also" (John 14:2-3).

Yes, you can KNOW that you are forgiven.
Accept Jesus as the only way to salvation...

Accepting Jesus as your Savior is not about what you can do, but rather about having faith in what Jesus has already done. It takes recognizing that you are a sinner, believing that Jesus died for your sins, and asking for forgiveness by placing your full trust in Jesus's work on the cross on your behalf.

God's Word says, "If you confess with your mouth that Jesus is Lord and believe in your heart that God raised him from the dead, you will be saved. For with the heart one believes and is justified, and with the mouth one confesses and is saved" (Romans 10:9-10).

Practically, what does that look like?
With a sincere heart, you can pray a simple prayer like this:

God,
I know that I am a sinner.
I don't want to live another day without embracing
the love and forgiveness that You have for me.
I ask for Your forgiveness.
I believe that You died for my sins and rose from the dead.
I surrender all that I am and ask You to be Lord of my life.
Help me to turn from my sin and follow You.
Teach me what it means to walk in freedom as I live under Your grace,
and help me to grow in Your ways as I seek to know You more.
Amen.

If you just prayed this prayer (or something similar in your own words), would you email us at info@lovegodgreatly.com?

We'd love to help get you started on this exciting journey as a child of God!

WELCOME FRIEND

We're so glad you're here

Love God Greatly exists to inspire, encourage, and equip women all over the world to make God's Word a priority in their lives.

INSPIRE
women to make God's Word a priority in their daily lives through our Bible study resources.

ENCOURAGE
women in their daily walks with God through online community and personal accountability.

EQUIP
women to grow in their faith, so that they can effectively reach others for Christ.

Love God Greatly consists of a beautiful community of women who use a variety of technology platforms to keep each other accountable in God's Word.

We start with a simple Bible reading plan, but it doesn't stop there.

Some gather in homes and churches locally, while others connect online with women across the globe. Whatever the method, we lovingly lock arms and unite for this purpose...to Love God Greatly with our lives.

At Love God Greatly, you'll find real, authentic women. Women who are imperfect, yet forgiven. Women who desire less of us, and a whole lot more of Jesus. Women who long to know God through his Word, because we know that Truth transforms and sets us free. Women who are better together, saturated in God's Word and in community with one another.

Love God Greatly is a 501 (C) (3) non-profit organization. Funding for Love God Greatly comes through donations and proceeds from our online Bible study journals and books. LGG is committed to providing quality Bible study materials and believes finances should never get in the way of a woman being able to participate in one of our studies. All journals and translated journals are available to download for free from LoveGodGreatly.com for those who cannot afford to purchase them. Our journals and books are also available for sale on Amazon. Search for "Love God Greatly" to see all of our Bible study journals and books. 100% of proceeds go directly back into supporting Love God Greatly and helping us inspire, encourage and equip women all over the world with God's Word.

THANK YOU for partnering with us!

WHAT WE OFFER:

18 + Translations | Bible Reading Plans | Online Bible Study
Love God Greatly App | 80 + Countries Served
Bible Study Journals & Books | Community Groups

EACH LGG STUDY INCLUDES:

Three Devotional Corresponding Blog Posts
Memory Verses | Weekly Challenge | Weekly Reading Plan
Reflection Questions And More!

OTHER LOVE GOD GREATLY STUDIES INCLUDE:

Savior | Promises of God | Love the Loveless | Truth Over Lies
1 & 2 Thessalonians | Fear & Anxiety | James | His Name Is...
Philippians | 1 & 2 Timothy | Sold Out | Ruth | Broken & Redeemed
Walking in Wisdom | God With Us | In Everything Give Thanks
You Are Forgiven | David | Ecclesiastes | Growing Through Prayer
Names of God | Galatians | Psalm 119 | 1st & 2nd Peter
Made For Community | The Road To Christmas
The Source Of Gratitude | Esther | You Are Loved

Visit us online at
LOVEGODGREATLY.COM

Made in the USA
Columbia, SC
07 November 2018